Rocky Mountain
National Park

impressions

photography and text by
Glenn Randall

FARCOUNTRY
PRESS

TITLE PAGE: Arrowleaf groundsel and mountain bluebells cluster along a timberline tributary of North St. Vrain Creek just above Lion Lake, with 13,310-foot Mt. Alice in the distance. This area, known as Wild Basin, has some of the best flower displays in the northern Front Range.

RIGHT: Taylor, Otis, and Hallett peaks and Flattop Mountain form a prominent part of the 25-mile stretch of the Continental Divide that lies in the Park. The spectacular aspen groves in the top right corner of the photo are growing on the Bierstadt Moraine, named, along with a nearby lake, for famed Western landscape painter Albert Bierstadt.

FRONT COVER: A leafless aspen grove on the flanks of Beaver Mountain welcomes the light of a stormy winter sunrise.

BACK COVER: Longs Peak, the Keyboard of the Winds, Pagoda Mountain, and Chiefs Head Peak are reflected in Bear Lake at sunset. Bear Lake is a "kettle" lake left behind when a large chunk of ice trapped in the moraine of a Pleistocene-era glacier melted.

ISBN 10: 1-56037-285-0
ISBN 13: 978-1-56037-285-1

For more information on our books, write Farcountry Press, P.O. Box 5630, Helena, MT 59604; call (800) 821-3874; or visit www.farcountrypress.com.

Created, produced, and designed in the United States. Printed in China.

17 16 15 14 13   3 4 5 6 7

Introduction

by Glenn Randall

$\mathcal{A}$t 1:00 A.M., my alarm wrenches me out of a restless sleep. My irritation vanishes as I remember why I set the alarm: I have a date with sunrise at 11,800 feet, and a long way to go to keep my commitment.

Minutes later, I'm on the road. Two mugs of strong coffee scour the dregs of sleep from my brain. At 2:30 A.M., I arrive at the Longs Peak Trailhead parking lot. The sign at the trailhead reads "9,400 feet." Already I'm half a mile higher than Mt. Mitchell, the highest point east of the Mississippi, and I haven't even left pavement. Rocky Mountain National Park has the highest altitude of any national park in the lower forty-eight states. One-third of its 265,769 acres lies above timberline. Sixteen peaks rise above 13,000 feet and one—14,255-foot Longs Peak—is part of the proud pantheon of Colorado's fifty-four "Fourteeners."

Although it's still three hours until sunrise on this July morning, the parking lot is nearly full. Hikers and mountaineers bustle about with last-minute preparations, laughing and talking, the beams of their headlamps stabbing through the night, then shoulder their packs and head up the trail. Roughly 27,000 people try to climb Longs Peak every year, mostly during July and August; about 60 or 70 percent succeed.

Climbing Longs Peak is a rite of passage for summit-starved residents of Front Range cities like Denver, Boulder, and Colorado Springs. Intense people-pressure from three million visitors each year has forced the park to strictly limit backcountry camping permits. That's why most Longs Peak aspirants attempt to blitz the mountain in just one day. Savvy mountaineers attempting Longs and all the other high peaks start well before dawn so they can reach the summit and return to the safety of timberline before the afternoon thunderstorms gather strength. Naive flatlanders who start after sunup often get hammered by rain, hail, and summer snow while still far above timberline. Too often they find themselves fleeing for their lives before the storm's wrath. Lightning, falls, and hypothermia have killed fifty-four mountaineers on Longs Peak since the park was created in 1915.

In years past, I would rise at 1:00 A.M. to tackle a demanding route on The Diamond, the vertical upper half of the east face of Longs Peak. Today, however, I leave the parking lot with fifty-five pounds of large-format camera gear on my back rather than ropes and rock-climbing hardware. My goal this July morning is not the summit but rather a photograph of sunrise at Chasm Lake, an icy pool nestled below the awesome east face of Longs. Reaching the lake, still 4.2 miles distant by trail, and 2,400 vertical feet higher, will take about two and a half hours of steady moonlit hiking. I labor upward, pondering the photographic possibilities.

Parry's primroses, named for nineteenth-century botanist Charles C. Parry, flower above Thunder Lake, in the Wild Basin area of the park. Parry's primroses have such a strong, musky odor that hikers sometimes smell them before they see them.

There won't be many flowers at Chasm Lake, that I know. Rocky Mountain National Park, unlike the Maroon Bells–Snowmass Wilderness Area near Aspen or the San Juan Mountains surrounding Silverton and Telluride, is not known for its wildflowers. The granitic soils are too poor, the rain too sparse, and the wind too strong to support the lush alpine gardens that adorn so many timberline meadows elsewhere in the state. The best flower fields lie hidden a day's hike into the wilderness. The timberline meadows surrounding Lion Lake, in Wild Basin, some 7 miles from the road, support lush fields of Indian paintbrush, arrowleaf groundsel, mountain bluebells, and heartleaf arnica, as do the meadows around the head-waters of East Inlet on the west side of the park. For the most part, however, the beauty of Rocky Mountain National Park lies in its pristine lakes, expansive areas of alpine tundra, and jagged peaks, which are far more rugged than many of Colorado's Fourteeners.

I reach timberline after a stren-uous hour. Still another hour and a half to go, pushing hard. Mercifully —and surprisingly—the wind is calm. Studies have shown that the wind speed in sum-mer on nearby Trail Ridge averages 48 mph with gusts up to 79 mph. Winter winds on Longs Peak are far worse, with average daily wind speeds on the summit of 65 mph. On one day out of five, wind speeds average over 100 mph, with peak gusts record-ed at 220 mph. Actually, 220 mph was only the highest wind speed recorded before the instrument blew apart. The true peak gust may have been still higher. Rocky Mountain National Park

Battling the spindrift pouring over Grace Falls, a frozen waterfall below Notchtop Mountain.

and the nearby Indian Peaks Wilderness possess the windiest mountains in Colorado.

Most strong winds in the park roar out of the west. In late winter and early spring, however, the wind sometimes changes direction com-pletely and flows, for a short time, out of the east. Weather forecasters call the conditions that produce such "upslope" flow a "Four Corners low." Low pressure aloft over the Four Corners region (where Utah, Colorado, Arizona, and New Mexico come together) produces low pressure at the sur-face in southeast Colorado. Winds spiral counter-clockwise around that low pressure center, drawing in abundant moisture from as far away as the Gulf of Mexico. If cold air is simultaneously flowing in from the north, the result can be a monster upslope storm. One of the biggest snowstorms ever recorded in Colorado dumped an estimated 80 inches of snow on the park's Bear Lake over three days in March 2003. I tried to snowshoe up a small peak called Emerald Mountain to photograph sunrise the day after the storm ended. It took me three exhausting hours to travel two-thirds of a mile, plowing a trench that, at times, was waist-deep even on snowshoes. After shooting moonset over the snow-plastered Continental Divide, I strolled down the path I had created and reached my truck again in a mere half an hour.

My thoughts return to the present as I reach the trail junc-tion leading to Chasm Lake. The sky is beginning to lighten to the east, and Longs Peak looms above me more clearly now, its summit curiously broad and flat. Geologists see that flat summit as a lingering remnant of the plain from which the current Rocky Mountains started rising about 38 million years ago. A much larger remnant of that plain can be seen along Trail Ridge Road, the highest point-to-point road in the nation, connecting Estes Park to the east and Grand Lake to the west. Trail Ridge Road crosses a broad expanse of rolling alpine tundra a few miles northwest of Longs Peak. The road, which is open only in summer, tops out at 12,183 feet—far above the nearest trees. In summer, large herds of elk roam the tundra alongside Trail Ridge Road, making this drive a must for both wildlife watching and soaking in the scenery. Come September and October, the elk descend to lower elevations. There, in Beaver Meadows, Horseshoe Park, and Moraine Park, the bulls gather harems of skittish females, "bugling" to drive away pesky rivals. A big bull's bugle is a haunting, never-to-be-forgotten sound. "If that doesn't stir your soul," said one visitor, "you don't have one."

Forty-five minutes before sunrise, I reach Chasm Lake. I still have plenty of time to dress warmly, find my composition, and set up my 4x5 field camera. For a moment I pause in the pre-dawn twilight, soaking in the grandeur of what is surely the most spectacular alpine cirque in Colorado. The glacier-carved east face of Longs Peak, composed of tawny Silver Plume granite about 1.4 billion years old, rises nearly vertically for 1,800 feet above Mills Glacier. The glacier was named for Enos Mills, an early mountain guide and naturalist who climbed Longs Peak over 300 times. Mills's tremendous love of the mountains near Estes Park made him the driving force behind the creation of Rocky Mountain National Park.

At last, sunrise bathes the soaring walls of Longs Peak in brilliant light, turning the granite orange. I meter and begin exposing film, scarcely drawing breath between exposures. Within a few fleeting minutes, the orange light fades to yellow, then to ordinary white. I pause in wonder, hoping the images do justice to the reality. This is why I came and why I've spent twenty-nine years exploring the spectacular beauty of Rocky Mountain National Park. I pack up, shoulder my load, and start the long journey back to my truck, and my home in Boulder, and sleep.

Mountain weather often ignores what's considered normal for the season. This 8-inch snowfall fell in early September—late summer according to the calendar. In the background rises 12,713-foot Hallett Peak, named for pioneer Colorado mountain climber William Hallett.

ABOVE: Columbine Falls, on the eastern slopes of Longs Peak, is bathed in golden light at the moment of sunrise. One of the Park's great attractions is the way unobstructed sunrise light flows across the flatlands of eastern Colorado and strikes the peaks rising abruptly above the plains.

LEFT: Twin Sisters and Estes Cone rise above the clouds shrouding the foothill valleys in this view from Windy Gulch. A weak upslope flow has pushed moist air in from the east. When the air hit the foothills it rose and cooled, and the moisture condensed into low-level clouds, leaving the higher peaks soaring into brilliant sunshine.

ABOVE: Longs Peak soars into the intense blue of a Colorado sky after an 18-inch snowfall temporarily closed many roads. The Park receives most of its heaviest snowfalls in March and April as upslope storms flow in from the east, sucking in moisture from as far away as the Gulf of Mexico.

RIGHT: Comet Hale-Bopp, the brightest comet of the twentieth century, sets over The Saber, which is illuminated by light from the first-quarter moon. It will be at least 2,400 years before Comet Hale-Bopp will once again be clearly visible from Earth.

ABOVE: An aspen branch, backlit by the rising sun, is silhouetted against Bear Lake.

RIGHT: 11,800-foot Chasm Lake, still thawing out in June, reflects the east face of Longs Peak, made golden by morning's light.

FAR RIGHT: The rising sun finds a momentary gap between gathering storm clouds and backlights an aspen grove on Beaver Mountain.

ABOVE: Lightning flashes over Eagle Cliff Mountain and The Crags along the eastern edge of the Park. In summer, afternoon lightning storms frequently pummel the high country.

FACING PAGE: Notchtop Mountain is reflected in Lake Helene at sunrise.

FACING PAGE: An April upslope storm dropped heavy snow over the Big Thompson River, already swelling with springtime snowmelt. The Big Thompson eventually flows into the Platte River, then to the Missouri and Mississippi rivers and the Gulf of Mexico.

BELOW: A white-tailed ptarmigan in winter plumage seems unconcerned about the gale-force winds sweeping Longs Peak near timberline. Male ptarmigan are the only birds that winter above timberline.

ABOVE: Heavy clouds block the bright, white light from the sky surrounding the sun, leaving an undiluted beam of intense pink and orange sunrise light to illuminate a cascade near Columbine Falls, on the eastern flank of Longs Peak.

RIGHT: The distinctive flat summit of Longs Peak rises above an icy wilderness in this sunrise view from Mt. Wuh. Wuh is the Arapaho Indian word for "grizzly bear."

RIGHT: A yellow-bellied marmot suns itself on the Continental Divide near Mt. Ida. Marmots gorge themselves all summer so they can hibernate all winter, their body temperature dropping to nearly 32 degrees F.

FACING PAGE: Longs Peak (the snowy peak on the far left), named for explorer Major Stephen Long, rises above Bear Lake in the springtime. In 1820 Long explored along the base of the Front Range, but he did not climb the peak that bears his name.

FACING PAGE: The photographer pauses to enjoy sunrise at Shelf Lake, reached by a rough, steep route leading out of Glacier Gorge that is marked by a few cairns.

BELOW: The growing season on the alpine tundra, frost to frost, is less than three months. These tiny tundra flowers growing near Trail Ridge Road measure barely a quarter-inch across.

ABOVE: Purple elephant's heads and yellow heartleaf arnica grace a subalpine wetland near Lion Lake, in the Wild Basin area. Chiefs Head Peak rises into the clouds beyond the timberline.

LEFT: Longs Peak rises nearly 6,000 vertical feet above Upper Beaver Meadows. In winter, powerful westerly winds nearly strip Longs Peak bare. In most years, a steady string of moist spring storms means that more snow crowns the peak in early June, when this photo was taken, than in January.

Dawn lights Columbine Falls and
the 1.4-billion-year-old Silver Plume
granite of Longs Peak.

ABOVE: This swirling cascade along the Big Thompson River near Moraine Park has trapped a few golden aspen leaves beneath the water's surface.

LEFT: Longs Peak, the Keyboard of the Winds, Pagoda Mountain, and Chiefs Head Peak form the distinctive skyline of Glacier Gorge, as seen from Bear Lake. Most snowstorms in the Park blow in from the west, with powerful winds that strip the trees and scour the windward slopes above timberline. Only gentle upslope storms, with winds from the east, create the winter wonderland captured here.

ABOVE: Chasm Meadow, at 11,600 feet, is a small green oasis beneath the rock-ribbed walls of Longs Peak.

RIGHT: Alpine sunflowers bloom near Trail Ridge Road as the afternoon cumulus begin to build over the Never Summer Range. Abundant displays like this one are rare because alpine sunflowers bloom and set seed just once after several years of vegetative growth and then die.

LEFT: At dawn a thin curtain of falling snow explodes into gold between the sun and the summit of Mt. Wuh.

BELOW: A glacial erratic is a boulder that has been moved by a glacier to a new location, then deposited when the glacier melted. This glacial erratic near Columbine Falls has been perched precariously there since the Pleistocene.

The spectacular Continental Divide skyline as seen at sunrise from Bierstadt Lake. (Left to right) Powell, Taylor, Otis, and Hallett peaks, and Flattop, Notchtop, and Knobtop mountains.

FACING PAGE: Aptly named Isolation Peak rises above the headwaters of East Inlet Creek on the west side of the Park.

BELOW: In springtime, every valley in the Park comes alive with the sound of falling water. This enchanting waterfall lies along North Inlet Creek on the west side of the Park, which usually receives more snow and hence more runoff than the east side.

LEFT: In the twilight just before sunrise, the sky glows lavender over Mt. Ypsilon, named for the Y-shaped gullies on its east face. Ypsilon is the Greek word for the letter Y.

BELOW: A rare calm morning allows Lake Verna, Spirit Lake, and Fourth Lake to reflect a sky aglow. The three lakes drain into Grand Lake, on the west side of the Park.

FACING PAGE: Skiing the north face of Longs Peak. A fall not checked immediately during this treacherous descent can lead to a fatal plunge over the vertical cliff called The Diamond.

BELOW: October marks the beginning of fall freeze-up. This swiftly flowing stream above Ypsilon Lake has not frozen solid yet, but the cold nights have frozen the splashing drops, forming an icy sculpture that would be the envy of a master glass-blower.

ABOVE: The late fall winds have kept most of Two Rivers Lake from freezing, but the cold air has blown thin sheets of ice up against the shore, where they reflect Notchtop Mountain at sunrise.

RIGHT: Isolation Peak rises above the beautiful flowers known by several common names: yellow fawn lilies, glacier lilies, avalanche lilies, or dogtooth violets. The scientific name is less in dispute: *Erythronium grandiflorum.*

BELOW: Alpine sunflowers bloom near Iceberg Pass, along Trail Ridge Road. The Never Summer Range rises in the distance, and in between lies Forest Canyon.

The east face
of Longs Peak,
bathed in the
dramatic light
of daybreak, is
reflected in
Chasm Lake,
still thawing
out in July after
a series of
spring storms
brought the
snowpack up
to 350 percent
of normal.

This ancient snag on Twin Sisters, most likely what is left of a limber pine, has weathered to a golden yellow. Sunrise amplifies the already warm tones and highlights Longs Peak, which rises behind.

RIGHT: Showy fields of columbine, like this one below Boulder–Grand Pass, are rare in the Park because of frequent high winds, relative dryness, and rocky soils.

BELOW: Columbine, the Colorado state flower since 1899, blooms prolifically near Fourth Lake, part of a chain of five lakes in the East Inlet drainage on the west side of the Park.

RIGHT: Notchtop Mountain and the Little Matterhorn catch light during a stormy sunrise. Snow-covered Odessa Lake can be seen through the trees.

BELOW: Longs Peak punctuates the Rocky Mountain National Park skyline, as seen from Steep Mountain at sunrise after an upslope snowstorm.

FACING PAGE: Winter slowly releases its grip on the high country. Odessa Lake starts to thaw in April, allowing the still water to capture the reflection of The Gable.

BELOW: Edmond Thomas Casey, a disciple of famed architect Frank Lloyd Wright, designed the Beaver Meadows Visitor Center, which is on the National Register of Historic Places. Longs Peak rises behind the visitor center.

From Timberline Pass, along the Ute Trail about 2 miles from Trail Ridge Road, the entire Rocky Mountain National Park skyline is revealed. From left to right, an experienced eye can pick out Longs Peak, Pagoda Mountain, Chiefs Head Peak, McHenrys Peak, Powell Peak, Taylor Peak, Hallett Peak, Flattop Mountain, and Notchtop Mountain.

FACING PAGE: The word "springtime" may evoke dainty visions of first flowers, but it is also a time for violent weather in the Park. Hikers caught above timberline by monster storms, like this one erupting over Longs Peak at sunset, should flee immediately for the safety of timberline.

BELOW: A mature bull elk intimidates a younger rival into retreating near the Ute Trail. Elk are the most commonly seen large mammals in the Park.

ABOVE: Spring thaw has started at Odessa Lake, allowing it to reflect Notchtop Mountain in its calm water.

LEFT: A thin shaft of pink sunrise light spotlights the Glacier Knobs while a late-spring storm wreathes the peaks of Glacier Gorge. The aspens surrounding Bear Lake have just started to leaf out.

ABOVE: Mt. Meeker, the second-highest peak in the Park at 13,911 feet, rises behind the chapel at Camp St. Malo, built in 1934. Joseph J. Bosetti, a young Catholic pastor who was also an avid mountaineer, was inspired to build a chapel and summer camp on the site when he witnessed a meteor appear to land in the woods at the foot of Mt. Meeker.

FACING PAGE: Early morning light reveals the sculpted forms of Sharkstooth, the Petite Grepon, and The Saber, all reflected in Sky Pond. The Petite Grepon, the "Eiffel Tower in stone" in the center of the skyline, is one of the most popular destinations in the Park for experienced rock climbers.

RIGHT: Arrowleaf groundsel and mountain bluebells soak in the drizzle alongside a stream flowing into Lion Lake #1, in the Wild Basin region. Upslope flow, with winds from the east, is primarily a late-winter and spring phenomenon, but it can bring moist, foggy conditions even in summer.

BELOW: Yellow heartleaf arnica and red Indian paintbrush bloom alongside this stream above Thunder Lake, in the Wild Basin region.

Water-loving
Parry's primrose
blooms soon
after the snow
melts away from
the shores of
Lion Lake #2, in
the Wild Basin
region.

The extraordinary red light on The Saber lasted just a minute as the rising sun found a tiny gap between dense clouds and the horizon. The dense clouds block the bright, white light from the sky around the sun, allowing the pure, undiluted red light of the sun to spotlight the jagged summit.

ABOVE: Running up the Tonahutu Creek Trail, heading toward Flattop Mountain and the Continental Divide on the west side of the Park.

FACING PAGE: The western flanks of many peaks in the Park are quite gentle, but The Cleaver, seen here rising above East Inlet Creek, is an exception.

FACING PAGE: Longs Peak is illuminated by the rising sun in this late-September view from Twin Sisters. Although the Park lacks the sprawling aspen groves of the mountains around Aspen and Telluride, the fall is still one of the most beautiful times of year.

BELOW: A bull elk, its antlers still swaddled in the "velvet" that supplies the growing antlers with blood, examines its surroundings warily. Heavy hunting pressure and competition with domestic livestock nearly led to the elimination of elk from the Park in the early 1900s. Today the well-protected elk herds are thriving.

ABOVE: A bighorn ram pauses to survey a visitor near Cow Creek, in the northeastern quadrant of the Park. Bighorn sheep were once common in the Park but have declined because of diseases transmitted by domestic livestock.

Participants in Ride the Rockies, a non-competitive cycling event that draws about two thousand participants every year, pedal over Trail Ridge Road.

Climbing the crux section of Diagonal Direct on the east face of Longs Peak. This is the most challenging wall in the Park for experienced rock climbers.

RIGHT: Clouds shaped like a cross section of a lens crown the Continental Divide to the right of Longs Peak, a sure sign of strong winds aloft. Further evidence of the prevailing westerlies can be seen in the large cornice in the top right corner of this image, taken at sunrise on Flattop Mountain.

BELOW: Soft pink light caresses Columbine Falls and Mt. Meeker at sunrise.

Hallett Peak dominates the skyline in the view west from Dream Lake. In summer, the surprisingly moderate routes on its steep northeastern face are a favorite destination for seasoned rock climbers.

FACING PAGE: Hallett Peak is reflected in Bear Lake at sunrise. The third week of September is typically the peak of fall colors.

BELOW: Trail Ridge Road, completed in 1932, gives even the most sedentary visitor easy access to the spectacular world above timberline. One of the most famous vistas along this fabled highway is the view of Longs Peak from the 12,120-foot Rock Cut.

ABOVE: During the fall rut, bull elk migrate from the high country down to lower-elevation meadows and even into the outskirts of Estes Park, causing "elk jams" as hordes of eager tourists stop to enjoy the spectacle.

RIGHT: Christmas lights adorn Elkhorn Avenue in downtown Estes Park as Hallett Peak rises into the pre-dawn twilight west of town. Estes Park is the gateway community for the east side of Rocky Mountain National Park.

RIGHT: Gossamer flakes of snow settle onto a boulder covered with orange crustose lichen along the trail to Lake Haiyaha. Lichens are a symbiotic combination of a fungus and an alga.

BELOW: The swirling patterns and weather-beaten texture in the wood of this ancient limber pine testify to the centuries it has endured along the shores of Lake Haiyaha.

One of the scenic climaxes of Rocky Mountain National Park is surely this view of Hallett Peak from Dream Lake, just a 1.2-mile hike from the Bear Lake parking lot. Although the view is always stunning, only rarely are visitors treated to this combination of perfect calm, ensuring a mirror-like reflection, and a brilliant sunrise.

Since 1979, Glenn Randall has combined his love of wilderness and adventure sports with a passion for photography. His intimate knowledge of the landscapes and sports he photographs allows him to find the intersections of magical light and stunning subject matter that produce exceptional images.

His work has been published in Audubon, Barnes & Noble, Sierra Club, Nature Conservancy, and *Runner's World* calendars and in *Audubon, GEO, Outdoor Photographer, Outside, Ski, Los Angeles Times Magazine, National Geographic Adventure, New York Times Magazine,* and many others. Prints of his landscape photographs can be found in galleries and gift shops across Colorado. His photographs have also been used in books published by Falcon Press, Lyons and Burford, New Readers Press, Reader's Digest General Books, and Scribner's.

All of Randall's landscape photographs are authentic records of truly memorable experiences in the backcountry. In addition to his photographic credentials, Randall is an accomplished writer who has authored seven books and more than 200 magazine articles, almost all about the outdoors.

For information about purchasing a print of any of the images in this book, please contact Glenn Randall at 303-499-3009 or gprandall@comcast.net.